CONTENTS

Bible Storyteller

T0022520

Session 1: Jesus Builds the Team

Session 2: Shiphrah, Puah, and Miram: God's Wonder Women

Session 3: Jethro Mentors Moses

Session 4: The Magnificent Magi

Session 5: Unexpected Heroes Give Paul a Basket Ride

Hero Hotline:
Called Together to Serve God!

	Bible Story	Hotline Tips	Music	Crafts
Session 1	Jesus Builds the Team John 1:35-51	Heroes are called to... Follow Jesus!	• Hero Hotline Theme Song • If U Wanna Be A Hero	• Hotline Comics • Hotline Cuff
Session 2	Shiphrah, Puah, and Miriam: God's Wonder Women Exodus 1:8–2:10	Heroes are called to... Help Others!	• Hold Up • Beat Like Yours	• Helping Hero Medal • Basket of Blessings
Session 3	Jethro Mentors Moses Exodus 18	Heroes are called to... Work Together!	• Let's Strive • Work Together	• Hero Puppet Team • Work Together Painting
Session 4	The Magnificent Magi Matthew 2:1-12	Heroes are called to... Listen to God!	• Good Good Life • Show Grace, Speak Truth	• Magi's Guiding Star • Hero Shield • Stars and Straws
Session 5	Unexpected Heroes Give Paul a Basket Ride Acts 9:1-25	Heroes are called to... Show Grace!	• Your Grace • That's What Makes A Hero	• Hero Team Frame

Hero Verse

So let's strive for the things that bring peace and the things that build each other up. (Romans 14:19)

Science	Recreation	Snacks	Notes
• Magnetic Attraction • Sinking Soda	• Hero Quick-Change • Heroic Catch • Hero Headquarters • Preschool Recreation	• Build Your Own Fig Tree • Super Vision Sticks • Nathanael's Fig Tree Fruit Bars	
• Bubbling Up • Super Straw	• Hero Helping Toss • Don't Wake the Baby • Practice Makes Heroes • Preschool Recreation	• Hope Heroes • Pretzel Power Lifts • Banana Boats	
• Power Paper • Super Bubble Blower	• Work Together Tag • Find the Team • Quickening Questions • Preschool Recreation	• Healthy Campfire • Campfire Trail Mix • Work Together Pizza	
• The Leak-Proof Bag • Looking for the Star	• Guided by a Star • Return Home Another Way • Heroic Attention • Preschool Recreation	• Colossal Courage Cookies • Veggie Treasures • Hero Ropes	
• Flying Ping-Pong Ball • Incredible Ice • Bonus Experiment: Liquid Light	• Grace Tag • Team Up! • Build a Basket • Preschool Recreation	• Marvelous Mini Cakes • Cones of Power • Basket Snacks	

Equipping Your Bible Story Station

Welcome to Hero Hotline: Called Together to Serve God!
Get your journey as Bible Storyteller off to a great start by following these simple pro tips:

- Attend all Hero Hotline leader training sessions to learn about the program and how your station fits into the overall message.

- Be prepared! Read through this book in its entirety, and practice the scripts multiple times with your team.

- Decorate your station (see pages 6–7 for ideas) and dress the part. Your Storyteller costume could be typical "Bible Times" attire: Robe, Tunic, Head Covering, and Ceinture. Modern attire also may work, especially when paired with a Hero Hotline T-Shirt, and maybe a Hero Hotline Cape.

- Collect supplies for each session well in advance. Keep a running list of borrowed items so you can easily return them. Get your congregation involved by publicizing a list of supplies to donate.

- **SAFETY TIP:** Ensure that your area is free of sharp objects and trip hazards.

- Check out the "VBS for Heroes with Special Needs" FREE resource at CokesburyVBS.com for tips on encouraging all Heroes to participate at their own levels of comfort.

- If it works for your group, play story-related songs from the Complete Music CD to help facilitate smooth transitions.

- Read "About This Resource" on page 5, but know that not every VBS needs to include every component of each session.

- Feel free to adapt any activities as best fits your group, space, and time allotment. Every church and program is unique, so make each session your own—and have fun with it!

About This Resource

From age-appropriate stories and conversations to energizing games and activities, each session is designed to engage multiple learning styles and encourage fun!

Setting the Scene

Immerse your Heroes in the Bible story with your stage. Decorate the stage area using the lists on page 6, as well as the tips for story-specific enhancements found at the beginning of each session.

Bible Background

Before you lead, go deep into the Bible story with contextual information on each story.

Story Starter

Introduce the story to your Heroes and say the Hotline Verse together in fun and memorable ways. You can use this before the Drama or the Single Storyteller option.

Bible Story Option 1: Drama

Invite your Heroes into the Bible story action with this dramatic skit option, adaptable for enactment by a team of volunteers, by Heroes reading the parts, or even by puppets. Please devote time to rehearsals—don't try to wing it! You may copy the pages of this section for use in rehearsal and performance.

Bible Story Option 2: Single Storyteller

Perfect for smaller classrooms, each of these scripts includes a complete telling of the Bible story with interactive enhancements to engage your Heroes' interest and encourage participation.

Life Application

How does the Bible story apply to the lives of your Heroes? Encourage them to explore this question with this guided recap and discussion. Invite time for multiple answers to each question. If your church does not use the Reflection Time Leader in another setting, consult this resource for additional questions.

Active Learning

Empower all of your Heros by employing multiple learning styles to reinforce each session's story.

Closing Prayer

Close each session with suggested age-appropriate prayers, or invite Heros to volunteer and pray their own.

Hotline Verse and Hotline Tip ASL

Demonstration photos for these are found in the "Free Resources" section at CokesburyVBS.com. Teach the body to help the mind remember with these American Sign Language interpretations of each session's Hotline Tip. See if you can memorize them all by the end of VBS! For a video tutorial of each sign, also check out the "Free Resources" section at CokesburyVBS.com!

Setting the Scene
Ready-to-Use Bible Story Station
Decorating Tools!

- Bible Story Station Activity Center Sign
- Bible Story Poster Pack
- Decorating Mobiles
- Decorating Poster Pack
- Decorating Transparencies (found in the **Decorating and Publicity Download** folder)
- Cave Wall Background
- Hero Hotline Large Logo Poster
- Purple Foil Fringe Curtain

- Logo String Flags
- Super Meer XL Character Poster
- Complete Music CD or MP3 tracks
- Scripture Treasure Lanyards
- Bible Storytelling Props (*see if you can re-use these hand-held props designed to cover stories from Knights of North Castle and Discovery on Adventure Island*)

Bible Story Station Setup To-Do List

- Place the Bible Story Station **Activity Center Sign** at your entrance.

- Design a fun focal wall where the Bible story action will take place. The Bible stories for Hero Hotline have both indoor and outdoor scenes. One half of the wall could represent "inside" and the other half "outside." Incorporate Bible-times set pieces, such as palm trees, rocks, jars, etc.

- Hang Hotline Tip and Hotline Verse **Decorating Posters**.

- Hang **Decorating Mobiles** at eye-catching levels.

- Check the first page of each session for story-specific scenes and materials.

- See the **Hero Hotline Decorating Guide** and **Decorating and Publicity Downloads** for more ideas.

When You Need to Adapt

Though we try to make the stories and activities in this resource accessible and useful to all, we understand your needs, program plan, and resources may vary. Here are some ideas that may be helpful for different settings.

- If you include your Preschool Heroes in rotation, consider using the "Experience the Bible Story" section of the **Hero Hotline Preschool/Kindergarten Leader** in addition to, or in place of, some of the activities in this book.

- Read the story straight from the Bible. Though Bible Story Options 1 and 2 offer engaging ways for Heroes to encounter the Bible story, consider reading or inviting some of your Heroes to read the story aloud from the Bible. *Note—as some biblical themes are more suited for mature audiences, pre-read each passage for content you may need to edit.

- Okay to copy: Some of our test churches invite Heroes to participate in the Bible Story Option 1 drama, either with a "readers' theater" approach or by acting out the story. In either case, feel free to make copies of any pages that include "Permission to photocopy this page is granted for local church use. © 2022 Abingdon Press. All rights Reserved" for this use.

- Spontaneous melodrama: Instead of using a large cast or individual readers, try the spontaneous melodrama approach. Assign roles to Heroes and have the Storyteller read all the parts aloud. Instruct Heroes to act out what is read for the role they have been assigned.

- Easy costume options: Some of our test churches have proven that costumes for Bible Storytelling don't have to be difficult. In many cases, a simple piece of card stock with a character's name on it is all you need. Have fun with it! If one person is playing multiple parts (e.g., Disciples 1 and 2, leaders 1 and 2), have their character card read "Disciples 1 and 2."

- If you don't have enough people to cover all of the roles in the drama, feel free to have your actors play multiple parts or combine parts. One of our test churches used the Bible Story Adventure Video in the Bible Storytelling station instead of Assembly time. Be sure and coordinate with your Assembly Leader if you make this adaptation.

Bible Story

Jesus Builds the Team
John 1:35-51

Hotline Verse

So let's strive for the things that bring peace and the things that build each other up.
(Romans 14:19)

Hotline Tip

Heroes are called to…
Follow Jesus!

Jesus Builds the Team
John 1:35-51

Materials
- Storyteller costume – could be modern attire, or all black, or a story shawl
- Bible-time attire for Peter, Philip, Nathanael, and Disciples 1 and 2 – tunics or robes
- Bible-time attire for Jesus – same as above but with a different color robe/tunic
- Beards optional
- Storyteller Stool and stand for Storyteller
- Sea of Galilee background
- Hero Hotline CD and CD player (or mp3 player)

Setting the Scene
- Designate one wall to be the focal wall, serving as the backdrop for the action.
- The wall can be decorated to give the feel of the Sea of Galilee in the background.
- The main staging area should be nice and open.
- The Storyteller's area could be to the side. There could even be a small story stool for the storyteller to sit on. Posted nearby, possibly directly overhead, could be the Hotline Verse – Romans 14:19 – So let's strive for the things that bring peace and the things that build each other up.
- Additionally, there could be space on a wall where each day's Hotline Tip can be posted as it is revealed. They would look great using the superhero comic book bursts (a la "POW," "BAM," etc.). Add the Hotline Tip signs each day so they fill up the wall by the end.

Bible Background

The Bible tells the story of God's love for us. The greatest expression of God's love is found in the person of Jesus and his ministry. The Old Testament of the Bible tells the story of God's people—the Israelites—from their beginning, through many generations of their history. The New Testament tells the story of Jesus, God's Son and a descendant of the Old Testament Israelites, as well as his ministry and the movement that arose from it.

Near the beginning of his ministry, Jesus called twelve people to be his disciples. Before they became Jesus' followers, several of them were disciples of a man named John the Baptist. John the Baptist was Jesus' relative and spent much of his own ministry preparing people to receive the message Jesus would bring. "Someone greater stands among you, whom you don't recognize. He comes after me, but I'm not worthy to untie his sandal straps" (John 1:26-27). John would later identify Jesus as "The Lamb of God, who takes away the sin of the world!" (1:29) and ultimately prompt his own disciples to leave him and follow Jesus.

The story of Jesus calling these disciples paints a picture of lifelong discipleship all in a few short moments. John the Baptist once again identifies Jesus as the Lamb of God and initiates a chain reaction leading his followers into a life of discipleship with Jesus. The disciples mentioned in this passage— Andrew, Simon, Philip, Nathanael, and an unnamed disciple (likely John, son of Zebedee)—deepen their insight into and understanding of who Jesus is as the story progresses. By the end of the account, they have acknowledged who Jesus is by the titles "Rabbi," "Messiah," "the one Moses wrote about in the Law and the Prophets," "God's Son," and "the king of Israel."

This passage highlights the role Jesus plays in the fulfillment of Israel's scriptures and the expectations Israel had for the Messiah. One of Jesus' new disciples, Philip, says, "We have found the one Moses wrote about in the Law and the Prophets: Jesus, Joseph's son, from Nazareth" (1:45). Philip understands that Scripture bears witness to Jesus as the Messiah, but Jesus takes this further and invites the disciples into the story. He mentions seeing Nathanael under a fig tree, an object that often represents Israel's struggle to remain faithful to God. Just as the disciples recognize Jesus' role in the story of God's people, Jesus invites them into the continuation of that story. We are extended that same invitation today.

Jesus calls all of us to be his disciples. Heroes respond to this call and follow him! A life of discipleship following Jesus helps us learn how to show God's love to other people. During Hero Hotline VBS, we will learn many ways to be a hero and share God's love. Responding to Jesus' call to follow him is our first step into a larger world. As you share this story with children, help them understand that the more we learn about Jesus and who he is, the better we can show God's love to other people like the disciples did!

Bible Story
Jesus Builds the Team
John 1:35-51

Hotline Verse
So let's strive for the things that bring peace and the things that build each other up.
(Romans 14:19)

Hotline Tip
Heroes are called to...
Follow Jesus!

Teacher Tip
This Bible Background feature is a supplemental aid provided for you, the Storyteller, to give context for each session's story before you teach on it. *You may share this information with your Heroes, if desired, but it is not a recommended portion of the intended lesson.*

Bible Story

Jesus Builds the Team
John 1:35-51

Hotline Verse

So let's strive for the things that bring peace and the things that build each other up.
(Romans 14:19)

Hotline Tip

Heroes are called to…
Follow Jesus!

Story Starter

Hello, Heroes! Welcome to Bible Story Headquarters. Here's where we'll explore stories of amazing heroes in a great book packed with heroes – the Holy Bible. Along the way we'll discover one of God's great truths – that heroes are called to serve God together.

Let's start with our key verse which is all about the power of striving together.

It's from Romans, chapter 14, verse 19, and goes like this –
So let's strive for the things that bring peace and the things that build each other up.

Repeat after me each line –
(Say each line then indicate for the Heroes to echo.)
So let's strive
for the things
that bring peace
and the things
that build each other up.

Wham! Bang! Pow! We're off to a great start!

Now it's time for our first Bible story. It's from the Gospel of John in the New Testament. *Gospel* is a word that means "good news," and this story is very good news. It's about Jesus calling the disciples.

Bible Story Option 1
Drama

Cast
- Storyteller
- Jesus
- Disciple 1
- Disciple 2
- Peter
- Philip
- Nathanael

Materials
- Storyteller Costume
- Backdrop for Story: A seaside, such as the Sea of Galilee
- Story stool at upstage right, or the Storyteller can remain standing off to the side
- Bible-time attire for Peter, Philip, Nathanael, and Disciples 1 and 2 – tunics or robes
- Bible-time attire for Jesus – same as above but with a different color robe/ tunic
- Beards optional

Bible Story
Jesus Builds the Team
John 1:35-51

Hotline Verse
So let's strive for the things that bring peace and the things that build each other up.
(Romans 14:19)

Hotline Tip
Heroes are called to…
Follow Jesus!

Storyteller: **John, who we often call John the Baptist, had told his followers about the greatness of Jesus. And then Jesus passed by…**
(Jesus enters and stands stage left. Disciples 1 and 2 enter stage right.)

Disciple 1: **There he is, the one John calls the Lamb of God.**

Disciple 2: **Which John? The one who will write all this down in the Gospels or John the Baptist?**

Disciple 1: **John the… wait, what's a "Gospel"?**

Disciple 2: **It means good news.**

Disciple 1: **Oh. Anyway, it's John the Baptist who calls him Lamb of God. You were there.**

Disciple 2: **And why is John called "John the Baptist"?**

Disciple 1: **Um, because he baptizes people.**

Disciple 2: **Oh right. Seems like that should be easy to remember.**

Disciple 1: **Come on. Let's follow him.**
(Jesus crosses from left to right, Disciple 1 and 2 follow behind. A sort of "follow-the-leader" ensues. Everything, Jesus does, the Disciples do – walk,

Bible Story
Jesus Builds the Team
John 1:35-51

Hotline Verse
So let's strive for the things that bring peace and the things that build each other up.
(Romans 14:19)

Hotline Tip
Heroes are called to…
Follow Jesus!

stop, stretch, scratch head, walk again)

Jesus: *(noticing that he's being followed)* **What are you looking for?**

Disciple 1: **Rabbi** *(to Disciple 2).* **That means teacher.**

Disciple 2: *(to Heroes)* **I knew that.**

Disciple 1: *(to Jesus)* **Rabbi, where are you staying?**

Jesus: **Come and see.**
(Jesus and Disciples 1 and 2 go and sit stage left as Storyteller narrates)

Storyteller: **So they went and saw where Jesus was staying, and they remained with him that day. It was about four o'clock in the afternoon.**

Disciple 1: *(standing)* **If you'll excuse me for a minute, I want to let my brother Simon know about all this.** *(stands and runs across to stage right and shouts to offstage)* **Hey Simon! Simon!**

Peter: *(we hear his voice from offstage)* **What is it?**

Disciple 1: **We have found the Messiah. "Messiah" means Christ.**

Peter: **I know what "Messiah" means.**

Disciple 1: **Right. Come on! I want you to meet him. Don't you want to meet him?!**

Peter: **Of course I do.** *(makes it onstage)* **Lead me to him.** *(Disciple 1 and Peter cross over to stage left; Jesus and Disciple 2 stand up)*

Jesus: *(to Peter)* **You are Simon, son of John. You will now be called Cephas.**

Disciple 1: *(whispering to Peter)* **"Cephas" is translated to Peter and that means "rock."**

Peter: **I know.**

Disciple 2: **"Rock"? Aw, man. I want a cool nickname, too.**
(Philip enters stage right. Jesus leads the way to stage right, followed by Peter, Disciple 1 and Disciple 2. Work in some more follow-the-leader movements.)

Storyteller: **The next day Jesus went into Galilee. He found Philip.**

Jesus: *(to Philip)* **Follow me.**

Philip: *(to Heroes)* **Jesus just asked me to follow him. Cool!** *(turns to call* *to Nathanael who is off stage right)* **Hey Nathanael, we have found the one Moses wrote about in the Law and the Prophets: Jesus, Joseph's son, from Nazareth.**

Nathanael: *(from offstage)* **Pfft. Nazareth?! Can anything from Nazareth be good?**

Philip: **Come and see.**
(Nathanael enters and stands stunned at the sight of Jesus)

Jesus: **Here is a genuine Israelite in whom there is no deceit.**

Nathanael: **H-h-how do you know me?**

Jesus answered: **Before Philip called you, I saw you under the fig tree.**

Nathanael: **Rabbi...**

Disciple 1: **Which means** *teacher.*

Peter, Philip, Nathanael, and Disciple 2: **We know.**

Nathanael: **You are God's Son. You are the king of Israel.**

Jesus: **Do you believe because I told you that I saw you under the fig tree? You will see greater things than these! I assure you that you will see heaven open and God's angels going up to heaven and down to earth on the Human One.**
(As Storyteller says last line, Jesus walks off stage right with Peter, Philip, Nathanael, and Disciples 1 and 2 following closely, doing everything he does – looking right, looking left, stopping to stretch etc.)

Storyteller: **Jesus called the disciples, and they followed him...** *(to the Disciples as they exit)***... but maybe not quite that close!**

Bible Story
Jesus Builds the Team
John 1:35-51

Hotline Verse
So let's strive for the things that bring peace and the things that build each other up.
(Romans 14:19)

Hotline Tip
Heroes are called to...
Follow Jesus!

Bible Story
Jesus Builds the Team
John 1:35-51

Hotline Verse
So let's strive for the things that bring peace and the things that build each other up.
(Romans 14:19)

Hotline Tip
Heroes are called to...
Follow Jesus!

Bible Story Option 2
Single Storyteller

Our Bible story for this session is a call-and-response story. Listen carefully. Every time you hear me talk about following, especially following Jesus, you respond like this:
(demonstrate as you also do the body motions)

We will follow *(stomp twice)*
Jesus. *(pat above knees twice)*
We will follow *(clap twice)*
Love. *(cross hands over heart – the sign for love.)*

(After demonstrating, have the Heroes do it with you.)
Great! Here we go!

John was standing again with two of his disciples. When he saw Jesus walking along he said, "Look! The Lamb of God! The two disciples heard what he said, and they followed Jesus.

We will follow
Jesus.
We will follow
Love.

When Jesus turned and saw them, he asked, "What are you looking for?" They said, "Rabbi (which is translated Teacher), where are you staying?" He replied, "Come and see." So they went and saw where he was staying, and they remained with him that day. It was about four o'clock in the afternoon.

One of the two disciples who heard what John said and followed Jesus –

We will follow
Jesus.
We will follow
Love.

This disciple was Andrew, the brother of Simon Peter. He first found his own brother Simon and said to him, "We have found the Messiah" (which is translated Christ). He led him to Jesus.

Jesus looked at him and said, "You are Simon, son of John. You will be called Cephas" (which is translated Peter).

The next day Jesus wanted to go into Galilee, and he found Philip. Jesus said to him, "Follow me."

We will follow
Jesus.
We will follow
Love.

Philip was from Bethsaida, the hometown of Andrew and Peter. Philip found Nathanael and said to him, "We have found the one Moses wrote about in the Law and the Prophets: Jesus, Joseph's son, from Nazareth."

Nathanael responded, "Can anything from Nazareth be good?"

Philip said, "Come and see." Philip led the way to Jesus, and Nathanael followed.

We will follow
Jesus.
We will follow
Love.

Jesus saw Nathanael coming toward him and said about him, "Here is a genuine Israelite in whom there is no deceit."

Nathanael asked him, "How do you know me?"

Jesus answered, "Before Philip called you, I saw you under the fig tree."

Nathanael knew then that Jesus was the one to follow.

We will follow
Jesus.
We will follow
Love.

Nathanael said, "Rabbi, you are God's Son. You are the king of Israel." Jesus answered, "Do you believe because I told you that I saw you under the fig tree? You will see greater things than these! I assure you that you will see heaven open and God's angels going up to heaven and down to earth on the Human One." Jesus had found his team, and they followed.

We will follow
Jesus.
We will follow
Love.

Bible Story
Jesus Builds the Team
John 1:35-51

Hotline Verse
So let's strive for the things that bring peace and the things that build each other up.
(Romans 14:19)

Hotline Tip
Heroes are called to…
Follow Jesus!

Bible Story

Jesus Builds the Team
John 1:35-51

Hotline Verse

So let's strive for the things that bring peace and the things that build each other up.
(Romans 14:19)

Hotline Tip

Heroes are called to…
Follow Jesus!

Life Application

The word disciple means "learner." When Jesus called the disciples, they followed. They were eager to learn from him. What is something you would like to learn from Jesus?

(Invite Heroes to respond.)

Disciples aren't just people who lived during Jesus's time on earth. By choosing to follow Jesus and learn from him, that makes you disciples too!

The disciples in the Bible story actually saw and heard Jesus physically call them. Jesus said "Come and see" and invited them along. What do you think Jesus' call to us might be like?
(Invite Heroes to respond. You might need to follow up by wondering aloud if Jesus's call would be something we could hear with our ears or if it might be more like a feeling in our hearts to do good and to help others.)

What are some of the qualities Jesus has that might make us want to follow him in the first place?
(Invite Heroes to respond. Some answers might include – "He rose for us." "He teaches us to love everyone." "He helps people." "He is kind and loving." "He is gentle and patient.")

Our Hotline Tip today is – Heroes are called to follow Jesus.

I'll say, "Heroes are called," and you respond with "to follow Jesus."
Ready? Here we go.
(Lead Heroes to respond to your call for the Hotline Tip.)

Wham! Bang! Pow! That was great!

Active Learning
Response Time

You will need several rulers.

SAY: **When Jesus called the disciples, they responded. How would each of us respond if called by Jesus? What would our "response time" be?**

Divide the Heroes into pairs *(or small groups).*

Have one in each pair hold the top of a ruler.

Have the other in the pair curl his/her/their fingers and thumb around the zero mark at the bottom but without touching the ruler.

Instruct the hero holding the ruler to let it drop without warning.

The other hero must try to catch it between the fingers and thumb.

If the hero catches it, have him/her/them check where the thumb ends up on the ruler.

Repeat this a few times and challenge the heroes to see if they can catch the ruler any quicker.

After a few tries have the heroes in each pair switch roles.

SAY: **You catch the ruler because a message travels from your eyes to your hand via your brain. There's a slight delay between the ruler dropping and you catching it while the message gets there. With practice, you can catch it more quickly, but there is a limit to how fast the message can travel. We might hear Jesus' call with our ears first, but that message needs to travel to our brains and to our hearts. What do you think Jesus is saying to you today?**

Bible Story
Jesus Builds the Team
John 1:35-51

Hotline Verse
So let's strive for the things that bring peace and the things that build each other up.
(Romans 14:19)

Hotline Tip
Heroes are called to…
Follow Jesus!

Bible Story
Jesus Builds the Team
John 1:35-51

Hotline Verse
So let's strive for the things that bring peace and the things that build each other up.
(Romans 14:19)

Hotline Tip
Heroes are called to...
Follow Jesus!

Closing Prayer
This is a call-and-response prayer.
Let's stand as we pray.
I'll say a part, and you will respond by walking in place as you say, "We want to follow Jesus."
(Practice once)

Let us pray.

Bible Storyteller: **Jesus calls us to follow him...**
All: **We want to follow Jesus.**

Bible Storyteller: **Even when times are tough...**
All: **We want to follow Jesus.**

Bible Storyteller: **Even when things get rough...**
All: **We want to follow Jesus.**

Bible Storyteller: **Even when days are dreary...**
All: **We want follow Jesus.**

Bible Storyteller: **Even when you feel weary...**
All: **We want to follow Jesus.**

Bible Storyteller: **And when everything is great...**
All: **We want to follow Jesus.**

Bible Storyteller: **And when joy overflows our plate...**
All: **We want to follow Jesus.**

Bible Storyteller: **Jesus calls us to follow him...**
All: **We want to follow Jesus.**

Shiphrah, Puah, and Miriam: God's Wonder Women
Exodus 1:8–2:10

Materials
- Storyteller costume – could be modern attire, or all black, or a story shawl
- Bible-time attire for Shiphrah, Puah, Miriam, and Moses' Mother – robes, sandals
- Headscarves, belts optional
- Attire for Pharaoh – more fancy headdress and robe with silver or gold
- Attire for Foreman – less fancy than Pharaoh, maybe without head dress, but still more fancy than the Hebrew women
- Storyteller Stool and stand for Storyteller
- Nile River background, perhaps some dried reeds or cattails in foreground
- Basket and baby doll
- Hero Hotline CD and CD player (or mp3 player)

Setting the Scene
- Designate one wall to be the focal wall, serving as the backdrop for the action.
- The wall can be decorated to give the feel of Egypt/Nile River in the background.
- The main staging area should be nice and open.
- The Storyteller's area could be to the side. There could even be a small story stool for the storyteller to sit on. Posted nearby, possibly directly overhead could be the Verse for the Week – Romans 14:19 – So let's strive for the things that bring peace and the things that build each other up.
- Additionally, there could be space on a wall where each day's Hotline Tip can be posted as it is revealed. They would look great using the superhero comic book bursts (a la "POW," "BAM," etc.). Add the Hotline Tip signs each day so they fill up the wall by the end.

Bible Story
Shiphrah, Puah, and Miriam: God's Wonder Women
Exodus 1:8–2:10

Hotline Verse
So let's strive for the things that bring peace and the things that build each other up.
(Romans 14:19)

Hotline Tip
Heroes are called to…
Help Others!

Bible Story
Shiphrah, Puah, and Miriam: God's Wonder Women
Exodus 1:8–2:10

Hotline Verse
So let's strive for the things that bring peace and the things that build each other up. (Romans 14:19)

Hotline Tip
Heroes are called to… Help Others!

Teacher Tip
This Bible Background feature is a supplemental aid provided for you, the Storyteller, to give context for each session's story before you teach on it. *You may share this information with your Heroes, if desired, but it is not a recommended portion of the intended lesson.*

Bible Background

The Book of Exodus in the Old Testament tells the story of God delivering God's people, the Israelites, from slavery in Egypt into a land God would provide for them. The journey to this Promised Land was long and began when God called a hero named Moses to lead the Israelites away. But Moses' story doesn't begin with his response to God's call—it began with some important women who saved Moses' life.

The Israelites had been in Egypt since the father of the people of Israel, Jacob, had moved with his family to find relief from famine. His family not only survived, but thrived, and their numbers continued to increase. They became so numerous, in fact, that after several generations of continued growth, the pharaoh in Egypt was worried that they would be a threat to his power.

In an attempt to eliminate this perceived threat, the pharaoh tried working the Israelites to death. But the Israelites became even more numerous, so the pharaoh ordered two midwives who assisted Hebrew mothers giving birth to kill any baby boy born to the Israelites. The two midwives charged with this task, Shiphrah and Puah, defied the pharaoh's order and refused to kill the Hebrew boys. They told the pharaoh that Hebrew women gave birth so quickly that no midwife could arrive in time to carry out the pharaoh's order!

These heroic women knew that their obedience lies ultimately with God—not Pharaoh. Without the cooperation of the midwives, Pharaoh turned to his own people to carry out his plan. He told them, "Throw every baby boy born to the Hebrew into the Nile River, but you can let all the girls live" (Exodus 1:22). But this time, even Pharaoh's own daughter disobeyed his order! An Israelite woman named Jochebed had hidden her son in a basket among some reeds in the river. Pharaoh's daughter heard the Hebrew child's cries and showed compassion, naming the child Moses and adopting him into Pharaoh's own household. And thanks to some quick ingenuity from the baby's sister, Pharaoh's daughter even paid Jochebed to nurse the boy, in stark contrast to the pharaoh's enslavement of the rest of the Israelites.

The Hebrew word used to describe the basket made by Jochebed is the same word used for the ark built by Noah in the Book of Genesis. In both instances, the word describes a vessel through which God provides deliverance. God delivers Moses from the pharaoh's decree, but in just a few years, God will use the boy who has been delivered to deliver all the Israelites from slavery in Egypt.

God calls us to be helpers. Heroes answer the call and help others! These women—Shiphrah, Puah, Jochebed, the pharaoh's daughter, and Moses' sister—opposed Pharaoh's violence against God's people. God consistently works through people who are disregarded by those in power to subvert that same power. At Hero Hotline VBS, we will learn how helping others shows people how much they matter to God, and how much good we can do when we work to help others together!

Story Starter

Hello, Heroes! Welcome back to Bible Story Headquarters. Yesterday we encountered a Bible story where someone called disciples to his team. Do you remember who that was?
(Invite Heroes to respond, "Jesus.")

For today's Bible story, we'll explore the Old Testament and things that happened way before the birth of Jesus. But first, let's get going with our Hotline Verse. You may remember, it's from Romans, chapter 14, verse 19, and goes like this –

So let's strive for the things that bring peace and the things that build each other up.

Now, since we're going back in time from the life of Jesus, let's do the verse backwards… sort of. Repeat after me each line:
(Say each line then indicate for the Heroes to echo.)

That build each other up.
And the things
That bring peace
For the things
So let's strive.

Whew! I don't know about you, but that gave me an ice cream headache. Let's try that forward once to get rid of the brain freeze.

Repeat after me:
(Say each line then indicate for the Heroes to echo.)
So let's strive
for the things
that bring peace
and the things
that build each other up.

Ah! Much better!

Now it's time for our Bible story. And this takes us back to ancient Egypt.

Bible Story
Shiphrah, Puah, and Miriam: God's Wonder Women
Exodus 1:8–2:10

Hotline Verse
So let's strive for the things that bring peace and the things that build each other up.
(Romans 14:19)

Hotline Tip
Heroes are called to… Help Others!

Bible Story

Shiphrah, Puah, and Miriam: God's Wonder Women
Exodus 1:8–2:10

Hotline Verse

So let's strive for the things that bring peace and the things that build each other up.
(Romans 14:19)

Hotline Tip

Heroes are called to... Help Others!

Pronunciation Guide

Shiphrah- shiff-rah
Puah- poo-ah

Bible Story Option 1
Drama

Cast

- Storyteller
- Shiphrah
- Puah
- Miriam
- Pharaoh
- Foreman
- Moses' Mother – nonspeaking role

Note: With a smaller cast, actors playing Shiphrah and Puah can also play Miriam and Moses' Mother... given a fairly quick costume change.

Materials:

- Storyteller costume – could be modern attire, or all black, or a story shawl
- Bible-time attire for Shiphrah, Puah, Miriam, and Moses' Mother – robes, sandals
- Headscarves optional
- Attire for Pharaoh – more fancy headdress and robe with gold or silver
- Attire for Foreman – less fancy than Pharaoh, maybe without headdress, but still more fancy than the Hebrew women
- Storyteller Stool and stand for Storyteller
- Nile River background, perhaps some dried reeds or cattails in foreground
- Basket and baby doll
- Hero Hotline CD and CD player (or mp3 player)

Storyteller: A new king came to power in Egypt who didn't know Joseph.
(Pharaoh and Foreman enter and go to center stage)

Pharaoh: *(irritated)* **Can you believe it? There are now more Israelites in Egypt than there are Egyptians! I mean, if we had a dodgeball game, they would have way more players than we would!**

Foreman: But dodgeball hasn't been invented yet, Pharaoh.

Pharaoh: *(ignoring)* **And if we put on a big Egyptian musical, I bet they'd get all the solos.** *(stamps floor a la a tantrum)* **Not fair!**

Foreman: We could force them to work. Then they would be too worn out to think they're better or stronger than us.

Pharaoh: Hey! I have an idea... We could force them to work. Then they would be too worn out to think they're better or stronger than us.

Foreman: *(exasperated but used to it)* **Brilliant as always, Pharaoh.**

Pharaoh: **Go and see that it is done.** *(Foreman exits stage right)* **We'll make the Israelites work hard, build storage cities, and maybe even a tree fort with a cool rope ladder for a certain Pharaoh. This is going to be great!** *(hops up and down gleefully)*

Storyteller: **But the more the Israelites were oppressed, the more their numbers grew.**

Foreman: *(re-entering stage right)* **Pharaoh, I've got some bad news.**

Pharaoh: **You mean, my brilliant plan isn't working?**

Foreman: **The Israelites are only growing stronger in number.**

Pharaoh: **But what about the…**

Foreman: **I'm sorry. No tree fort.**

Pharaoh: *(hopping mad – literally)* **That does it! No more "Mister Nice Pharaoh"! We will make the Israelites our slaves. They will do hard work – make bricks, field work, really hard stuff!**

Foreman: **I will see that it is done.**

Pharaoh: **Good! And send in those two Hebrew women Shiphrah and Puah.** *(Foreman exits. Shiphrah and Puah enter stage right)*

Shiphrah: **You sent for us, Pharaoh?**

Pharaoh: **Yes. You two are Shiphrah and Puah, right?**

Shiphrah and Puah: **Right.**

Pharaoh: **The ones who are very helpful when babies are born, right?**

Shiphrah and Puah: **Right.**

Pharaoh: **Great! I have a job for you. When you are helping Hebrew babies be born, if it's a baby girl, that's fine. But if it's a baby boy… get rid of it.**

Puah: **By "get rid of it" you mean taking it to a loving family, right?**

Pharaoh: **I mean** (with a menacing tone) **Get rid of it.**
(Shiphrah and Puah gasp in shock)

Pharaoh: **That is my order. And I'm the Pharaoh. So, get to it!**
(Shiphrah and Puah walk down stage right to talk to each other out of ear-shot of Pharaoh)

Bible Story
Shiphrah, Puah, and Miriam: God's Wonder Women
Exodus 1:8–2:10

Hotline Verse
So let's strive for the things that bring peace and the things that build each other up.
(Romans 14:19)

Hotline Tip
Heroes are called to… Help Others!

Pronunciation Guide
Shiphrah- shiff-rah
Puah- poo-ah

Bible Story

Shiphrah, Puah, and Miriam: God's Wonder Women
Exodus 1:8–2:10

Hotline Verse

So let's strive for the things that bring peace and the things that build each other up.
(Romans 14:19)

Hotline Tip

Heroes are called to… Help Others!

Shiphrah: **We can't do that! We are people of God.**

Puah: **But if we don't, Pharaoh will be mad. We'd better think of something.**

Storyteller: **Of course, Shiphrah and Puah could never carry out Pharaoh's command. And he was not happy about it.**

Pharaoh: **Shiphrah! Puah!**
(Shiphrah and Puah return to center stage near Pharaoh.)

Shiphrah and Puah: **Yes, Pharaoh?**

Pharaoh: **My messengers have told me that even more Hebrew boys are being born! How can this be?**

Puah: **Well, Pharaoh, we're doing our best… but… um… it seems that Hebrew children are really good at being born, and by the time we arrive, there's nothing we can do.**

Pharaoh: **That's it. That's the last straw. From here on out, I give an order to all my people… that any baby boy born to the Hebrews be thrown into the Nile River!**

Shiphrah: **But Pharaoh, there are crocodiles in the Nile!**
Pharaoh: **I know!** *(exits stage right)*

Puah: **Come on, Shiphrah. Let's see what else we can do to help our people.**
(Shiphrah and Puah exit stage left.)

Storyteller: **During the time when this was happening, a certain couple devoted to God had a child, a son. The child's mother saw that he was beautiful and healthy, but also in danger because of Pharaoh's order. So she hid the child.**
(Moses' Mother enters stage left and pantomimes action as Storyteller narrates. Miriam enters as well.)

But after three months she could not hide her son any longer. She took a reed basket and made it waterproof. She put her child in the basket and set it among the reeds in the riverbank. The baby's older sister, Miriam, stood watch nearby.
(Moses' Mother exits stage left while Miriam remains and crouches low. Pharaoh's Daughter enters stage right.)

Miriam: **That's Pharaoh's own daughter. It looks like she's coming down to the river to bathe. She'd better watch out for crocodiles. Come to think of it, I'd better watch out for crocodiles.**

Pharaoh's Daughter: *(seeing the basket)* **What a lovely basket. Someone must** have lost it. *(surprised)* **And there's a baby inside! This must be one of the Hebrews' children.** *(picks up baby, holding it gently and rocking it)* **There, there. I've got you. If only I had someone who could help me take care of you.**

Miriam: **Ahem. If you like, I can find just the right woman to help you.**

Pharaoh's Daughter: **That would be lovely. Thank you so much.**

Miriam: **I'll be right back.** *(runs over to stage left and stage whispers)* **Mother. Mother, come here. I've got a wonderful surprise for you.**
(Moses' Mother enters. Miriam takes her by the hand to Pharaoh's Daughter)

Miriam: **I know this woman very well. She will be the perfect person to help you take care of the child.**

Pharaoh's Daughter: **How wonderful!** *(hands baby to Moses' Mother, who holds him with expert care)* **Here, if you will help me care for him, I will even pay you for your work. Come.** *(Pharaoh's Daughter and Moses' Mother walk off stage right while Miriam waves)* **You shall be my son, and I will name you Moses because I pulled you out of the water.**

Storyteller: **Thanks to Shiphrah, Puah, and Miriam – God's Wonder Women – Moses' life was saved. He would also go on to be a great hero for God's people. But that's another story…**

Bible Story Option 2
Single Storyteller

Our Bible story for this session is an Amen!/Aw, man story. Every time you hear good, uplifting, or positive news, say, "Amen"! And every time you hear something sad or tough, say, "Aw, man."

Ready? Here we go!
Note: Use inflection to really signal to the Heroes whether their response should be "Amen!" or "Aw, man." If heroes seem to miss it, you could also signal with a thumbs up or thumbs down.

A new king, Pharaoh, came to power in Egypt. He didn't care about Joseph and was worried about how many Israelites were in Egypt. He decided to harass them with forced labor and hard work.

Aw, man.

But even though the Israelites were oppressed, their numbers grew.

Amen!

So, the Egyptians decided to completely enslave the Israelites, making them do all kinds of cruel work.

Aw, man.

During that time, there were two Hebrew women, Shiphrah and Puah, who were very helpful in making sure babies were born safely, and their mothers were cared for.

Amen!

But Pharaoh instructed them that if they encountered a Hebrew boy being born, they were to do away with the baby.

Aw, man.

Shiphrah and Puah did a brave and risky thing. They disobeyed Pharaoh and made sure the baby boys lived.
Amen!

This was pleasing to God, but very displeasing to Pharaoh. He gave an order, "Throw every baby boy born to the Hebrews into the Nile River."

Aw, man.

Bible Story
Shiphrah, Puah, and Miriam: God's Wonder Women
Exodus 1:8–2:10

Hotline Verse
So let's strive for the things that bring peace and the things that build each other up.
(Romans 14:19)

Hotline Tip
Heroes are called to…
Help Others!

Pronunciation Guide
Shiphrah- shiff-rah
Puah- poo-ah

Adaptation
Go to the "Free Resources" tab at www.cokesburyvbs.com and download the happy face/sad face template. Print on for each Hero, then adhere to each side of a jumbo craft stick. Instruct Heroes to show you the happy face for happy news and the sad face for sad news.

One couple had a son, and they saw that the baby was healthy and beautiful.

Amen!

But after three months, his mother knew it was too dangerous for her to hide him much longer.

Aw, man.

She took a reed basket and sealed it with black tar. She put the child in the basket and set the basket among the reeds at the riverbank. The baby's older sister, Miriam, stood watch nearby.

Amen!

Pharaoh's daughter came down to bathe in the river, while her women servants walked along beside the river. She saw the basket among the reeds, and she sent one of her servants to bring it to her. When she opened it, she saw the child. The boy was crying.

Aw, man.

She felt sorry for him and said, "This must be one of the Hebrews' children." Then the baby's sister, Miriam, said to Pharaoh's daughter, "Would you like me to go and find one of the Hebrew women to nurse the child for you?" Pharaoh's daughter agreed, "Yes, do that."

Amen!

The girl went and called the child's mother. Pharaoh's daughter said to her, "Take this child and care for it for me, and I'll pay you for your work."

Amen!

So the woman got to care for her own child. After the child had grown up, she brought him back to Pharaoh's daughter, who adopted him as her son. She named him Moses, "because," she said, "I pulled him out of the water."

Amen!

Bible Story
Shiphrah, Puah, and Miriam: God's Wonder Women
Exodus 1:8–2:10

Hotline Verse
So let's strive for the things that bring peace and the things that build each other up.
(Romans 14:19)

Hotline Tip
Heroes are called to… Help Others!

Bible Story

Shiphrah, Puah, and
Miriam: God's Wonder
Women
Exodus 1:8–2:10

Hotline Verse

So let's strive for the
things that bring peace
and the things that build
each other up.
(Romans 14:19)

Hotline Tip

Heroes are called to…
Help Others!

Life Application

This is a story of really brave women helping others. Shiphrah and Puah were Hebrew women who helped any time a baby was born. How did they help the Hebrew babies?

(Invite Heroes to respond. Shiphrah and Puah disobeyed Pharaoh's orders by not getting rid of any Hebrew baby boys. They followed God's way, which was right, but also risky because Pharaoh was not happy.)

When Moses was born, how did his older sister Miriam help?

(Invite Heroes to respond. Miriam watched over him in the river. When Pharaoh's daughter pulled him out of the water, Miriam quickly suggested that Moses' own mother help care for the child.)

Even Pharaoh's daughter chose to be helpful. How?

(Pharaoh's daughter didn't see baby Moses as an "outsider" or a problem to be dealt with, but as a child who needed care. She adopted him as her own son.)

Divide the Heroes into small groups.

When was a time you helped someone (or an animal/pet) in need?

(Invite Heroes to discuss in their small groups. Ensure everyone who chooses to gets to share.)

Our Hotline Tip for today is - Heroes are called to help others.

Let's help each other out in chanting it. I'll say the first word. Then you help by adding the second word, and so on. Here we go.

Heroes
(Encourage Heroes to say "are.")

Called
(Heroes say "to")

Help
(Heroes say "others")

Great! Now this time, you start by saying "Heroes." Go!
(facilitate this)

Wham! Bang! Pow! That was great!

Active Learning
Helping Hands

Set up a table with a few props such as:
- A hair brush
- Hand mirror
- A hat or two
- Piece of paper and crayon
- Assorted blocks
- Fake flower

SAY: **Moses grew to become a great leader for God's people. He led God's people out of slavery in Egypt. He received the Ten Commandments from God on Mount Sinai. But before any of that could happen, Moses started out as a little baby... who needed helping hands to protect him and care for him.**

Choose one Hero to be the body. This Hero will put their hands behind their back.

Choose a second Hero to stand behind the first and place their arms through the first Hero's bent elbows to create the illusion that the arms belong to the first Hero.

The two must work together to maintain the illusion.

The Hero in front, the "body" must justify whatever the hands do by using appropriate dialogue.

The reverse is also true – if the "body" Hero starts talking about doing something, the "hands" Hero needs to match.

A third Hero can serve as the "helper" to help motivate the body and hands by asking them to do things. For example:

Helper: **Oh. I see you have a piece of paper and a crayon. Are you an artist?**

Hero 1: **Yes I am. Would you like me to make you a picture?**

Helper: **Sure!**

Hero 1: *(while hands Hero fumbles around for crayon)* **Let me see. Where did I put that crayon?** *(and so on)*

If time allows, give each Hero a chance to play the body, the hands, and the "helper" role.

Bible Story
Shiphrah, Puah, and Miriam: God's Wonder Women
Exodus 1:8–2:10

Hotline Verse
So let's strive for the things that bring peace and the things that build each other up.
(Romans 14:19)

Hotline Tip
Heroes are called to... Help Others!

Bible Story

Shiphrah, Puah, and
Miriam: God's Wonder
Women
Exodus 1:8–2:10

Hotline Verse

So let's strive for the
things that bring peace
and the things that build
each other up.
(Romans 14:19)

Hotline Tip

Heroes are called to…
Help Others!

Closing Prayer:

Repeat after me each line of this echo prayer.

I may be young.
I may be small.
But I can listen
To God's call.

I will follow.
God will lead
As I help
All those in need.
Amen.

Jethro Mentors Moses
Exodus 18

Materials
- Storyteller costume – could be modern attire, or all black, or a story shawl
- Bible time attire for Zipporah – Tunic or robe – headscarf optional
- Bible-time attire for Jethro, Israelites 1 and 2 – tunics or robes
- Bible-time attire for Moses – same as above but with a different color robe/tunic and possibly a walking staff
- Beards optional – but would work especially well for Jethro and Moses
- Bible time attire for Gershom and Eliezer – could be same as for Jethro and Israelites 1 and 2 however… in this version, Gershom and Eliezer were written young, almost school children age, so anything that makes them appear younger is a bonus
- Storyteller Stool and stand for Storyteller
- Background - Mount Sinai, perhaps some desert scrub brush and rocky terrain
- Hero Hotline CD and CD player (or mp3 player)

Setting the Scene
- Designate one wall to be the focal wall, serving as the backdrop for the action.
- The wall can be decorated to give the feel of Mount Sinai in the background.
- The main staging area should be nice and open.
- The Storyteller's area could be to the side. There could even be a small story stool for the storyteller to sit on. Posted nearby, possibly directly overhead could be the Verse for the Week – Romans 14:19 – So let's strive for the things that bring peace and the things that build each other up.
- Additionally, there could be space on a wall where each day's Hotline Tip can be posted as it is revealed. They would look great using the superhero comic book bursts (a la "POW," "BAM," etc.) Add the Hotline Tip signs each day so they fill up the wall by the end.

Bible Story
Jethro Mentors Moses
Exodus 18

Hotline Verse
So let's strive for the things that bring peace and the things that build each other up.
(Romans 14:19)

Hotline Tip
Heroes are called to… Work Together!

Pronunciation Guide
Zipporah-zuh-paw-ruh
Gershom- gur-shuhm
Eliezer- eh-lee-ay-zr

Bible Story
Jethro Mentors Moses
Exodus 18

Hotline Verse
So let's strive for the things that bring peace and the things that build each other up.
(Romans 14:19)

Hotline Tip
Heroes are called to…
Work Together!

Teacher Tip
This Bible Background feature is a supplemental aid provided for you, the Storyteller, to give context for each session's story before you teach on it. *You may share this information with your Heroes, if desired, but it is not a recommended portion of the intended lesson.*

Bible Background

We learned in Session 2 that the Book of Exodus tells the story of God delivering God's people from slavery in Egypt. What began with several women working together to save boys born to Hebrew women continued with Moses leading the Israelites out of Egypt. Before arriving in the land God would provide for them, the Israelites spent a considerable amount of time in the desert—particularly at a place called God's mountain (also called Mount Sinai or Mount Horeb), where our story takes place.

Between the time he was adopted into the pharaoh's household as a young child and when he led the Israelites out of Egypt, Moses spent time in a place called Midian, where he had married a woman named Zipporah. Zipporah was the daughter of Jethro, who was a Midianite priest. Zipporah and Moses had two sons, Gershom and Eliezer. As the events of the Israelites' departure from Egypt unfolded, however, Moses sent his family to live with Jethro. Now Jethro has brought Moses' family back to him at this camp on God's mountain.

Moses was charged as the leader of the Israelite people and had been leading them single-handedly. Jethro witnessed Moses presiding over the people on his own and advised Moses against doing it all on his own. "What you are doing isn't good. You will end up totally wearing yourself out, both you and these people who are with you" (Exodus 18:17-18). The Hebrew word for "wearing yourself out" literally means "to wither." This idea of "withering" would be immediately understood by agricultural societies who heard it. In today's more technological societies, a different word is more widely understood: "burnout." Jethro is hoping to spare Moses from burning out.

Jethro gives Moses advice: Bring the people's disputes before God, explain God's regulations and instructions to the people, and seek out capable helpers to lead the Israelites. Invite those leaders to judge minor disputes so that Moses can be free to judge the more difficult ones. Jethro also tells Moses to make sure that the advice he gives the Israelites matches up with what God commands. He reminds Moses that God's acts in Egypt demonstrate God's supremacy over any other gods, and that the ultimate source for judicial insight is God. But Jethro also understands Moses' call to be God's intercessor for the Israelites, and this lays the foundation for Moses to be the one who gives God's law to the Israelites later in the Book of Exodus.

God doesn't want us to wither or burn out. God knows we can accomplish great things when we team up! Heroes respond to God's call to work together. Jethro taught Moses this important lesson, and the Israelites move forward with their new method of governance. Through the encounter, we are given a great example of how being a hero means working together. At Hero Hotline VBS, we learn how much good we can do when we work as a team!

Story Starter

SAY: **Hello, Heroes! We've reached the midpoint of our time together this week. And things are moving fast. That little baby in the basket from yesterday… now what was his name again?** *(Invite the Heroes to respond, "Moses.")*

Moses, right! Because he was drawn out of the river. Do you remember why he was placed in the river in the first place? *(Invite Heroes to answer, "His mother put him in a basket on the Nile River to keep him safe." "Pharaoh wanted to get rid of him." Etc.)*

Right. A lot of Wonder Women did their part to keep baby Moses safe – Shiphrah and Puah, Moses' mother, Moses' sister Miriam, even Pharaoh's daughter. And guess what? I wonder whatever happened to that baby in the basket. We're about to find out. But before we do, let's remember our verse for the week - Romans chapter 14, verse 19, which goes like this –

So let's strive for the things that bring peace and the things that build each other up.

Let's help each other say the verse today in a game called One Word at a Time. Here's how it works. I'll say the first word of the Bible verse, then you say the second, I'll say the third, and so on. Let's start slowly.

Guide the Heroes though this, alternating words.

So (Storyteller)
let's (Heroes)
strive
for
the
things
that
bring
peace
and
the
things
that
build
each
other
up.

Let's do that one more time, a little faster.
(Facilitate this once again.)

Wham! Bang! Pow! You are really good at that! And now it's time for our Bible story.

Bible Story
Jethro Mentors Moses
Exodus 18

Hotline Verse
So let's strive for the things that bring peace and the things that build each other up.
(Romans 14:19)

Hotline Tip
Heroes are called to… Work Together!

Pronunciation Guide
Zipporah-zuh-paw-ruh
Gershom- gur-shuh m
Eliezer- eh-lee-ay-zr

Adaptation
Turn saying the Hotline Verse into a game. Sit in a circle and clap, clap, then pat, pat (on knees) to keep the rhythym. Say one word per clap or pat, as follows:
So (clap, clap)
let's (pat, pat),
and so on.
If a word is missed, start back at the beginning of the verse with the next verse until you get the whole verse.

Bible Story

Jethro Mentors Moses
Exodus 18

Hotline Verse

So let's strive for the things that bring peace and the things that build each other up.
(Romans 14:19)

Hotline Tip

Heroes are called to…
Work Together!

Pronunciation Guide

Zipporah-zuh-paw-ruh
Gershom- gur-shuh m
Eliezer- eh-lee-ay-zr

Bible Story Option 1
Drama
Cast

• Storyteller
• Moses
• Jethro
• Zipporah – Moses' Wife
• Gershom – Moses' and Zipporah's Child
• Eliezer – Moses' and Zipporah's Child
• Israelite 1
• Israelite 2

Note: With a smaller cast, Israelites 1 and 2 can be played by actors who also play Zipporah, Gershom, or Eliezer

• Storyteller costume – could be modern attire, or all black, or a story shawl
• Bible time attire for Zipporah – Tunic or robe – headscarf optional
• Bible-time attire for Jethro, Israelites 1 and 2 – tunics or robes
• Bible-time attire for Moses – same as above but with a different color robe/tunic and possibly a walking staff
• Beards optional – but would work especially well for Jethro and Moses.
• Bible time attire for Gershom and Eliezer – could be same as for Jethro and Israelites 1 and 2 however… in this version, Gershom and Eliezer were written young, almost school children age, so anything that makes them appear younger is a bonus
• Storyteller Stool and stand for Storyteller
• Background : Mount Sinai, perhaps some desert scrub brush and rocky terrain

(Moses walks to center stage while Storyteller narrates)
Storyteller: **Baby Moses, that baby in the basket who was drawn from the water, grew up to lead God's people out of slavery in Egypt. Here we find Moses in the desert at the base of Mount Sinai – God's mountain.**

Jethro: *(entering from stage right)* **Moses? Is that really you?**

Moses: **My Father-in-Law, Jethro! It's been too long. Where are Zipporah and the kids?**

Jethro: **They were right behind me. I think Eliezer got distracted looking at a camel.**
(Zipporah, Gershom, and Eliezer enter from stage right)

Eliezer: **I was sure I spotted one this time.**

Gershom: **For the last time, there's no such thing as a camel with no humps. What you saw was a donkey.**

Zipporah: **Kids, enough arguing. There's your father.**

Gershom and Eliezer: *(excited)* **Dad!** *(they both run over to hug Moses)*

Moses: **Gershom! Eliezer! It's great to see you.**

Gershom: **How was your business trip father?**

Moses: **I was doing God's work, but I'm not sure I would call it a "business trip."**

Eliezer: **Did you bring back any cool souvenirs like a t-shirt that says, "I Heart Camels?"**

Moses: **No. But I did lead God's people out of slavery in Egypt, through the Red Sea to here. Maybe that can be enough for one trip?**

Zipporah: **It's more than enough. Um… did you say through the Red Sea?**

Moses: **Yes. Pharaoh's army came after us in their chariots. But the Lord divided the waters of the Red Sea and the wind made the ground dry. All the Israelites made it all the way through, but just when Pharaoh's army was about to catch up, whoosh! The water came rushing back, and we were saved!**

Gershom and Eliezer: **Cool!**

Eliezer: **Hey, do you think a camel could pull a chariot?**

Gershom: **Enough with the camels!**

Zipporah: *(shushing them)* **Ssh. Moses, please tell me you'll get to take some time to rest now.**

Moses: *(sighs)* **I will at some point, Zipporah. But for now, I still have so much work to do for God and God's people.**

Zipporah: **Well, at least we're all together again.**

Moses: *(sincerely)* **Thank God for that.**

Zipporah: **Gershom, Eliezer, let's get a little something to eat. I think your father and grandfather have some things to discuss.**
(Zipporah, Gershon, and Eliezer exits stage right)

Jethro: **Moses, you truly are a wonderful son-in-law. To think of all you've been through, and what God has done on Israel's behalf. Now I know that the Lord is greater than all the gods.**

Bible Story
Jethro Mentors Moses
Exodus 18

Hotline Verse
So let's strive for the things that bring peace and the things that build each other up.
(Romans 14:19)

Hotline Tip
Heroes are called to…
Work Together!

Bible Story
Jethro Mentors Moses
Exodus 18

Hotline Verse
So let's strive for the things that bring peace and the things that build each other up.
(Romans 14:19)

Hotline Tip
Heroes are called to…
Work Together!

(As Storyteller narrates, chair is brought in. Moses sits front and center. Israelites 1 and 2 enter stage left)

Storyteller: **The next day Moses sat as a judge for the people, while the people stood around Moses and brought their disputes to him from morning until evening.**

Moses: **What is your dispute?**

Israelite 1: **Moses, last night before dinner his/her/their eyes were open during the blessing.**

Israelite 2: **Oh yeah? Well, how would you know unless your eyes were open, too?**

Israelite 1: **So you're saying your eyes were open.**

Israelites 1 and 2: **Moses?!**

Moses: *(tired)* **It's okay to have your eyes open during the blessing. What's more important is to remember to be a blessing to one another.**

Israelites 1 and 2: *(sheepishly)* **Yes, Moses.**
(Israelites 1 and 2 exit stage left as Jethro enters stage right)

Jethro: **Moses, what are you doing? Are you really sitting alone, trying to solve all the people's disputes on your own? You'll be here forever!**

Moses: **The people look to me. When there's a conflict, they bring it to me and I judge the best I can. I also teach them about God's law. What am I to do?**

Jethro: **Moses, this much work is too much for one person. It's not healthy. You know, self-care isn't selfish.**

Moses: **What do you mean?**

Jethro: **If I can give you some gentle advice, and may God be with you. You should continue teaching the people God's way and settling major disagreements.**

Moses: **I feel like I'm doing that already.**

Jethro: **You are. But you should also share the load! Find capable people who respect God. Set these people to listen to disputes. Let them bring the big disputes to you. But the little disputes, they can handle those. This will be much easier for you.**

Moses: **Do you think that will work?**

HERO HOTLINE: Called Together to Serve God!

Jethro: **If you do this and God directs you, then you will be able to endure. And all these people will be able to go back to their homes much happier. Moses, we need you. Your wife and children need you. And God needs you. And what we need most is to make sure you don't work so hard now, there's nothing left of you later. Share. The. Load.**
(Moses nods. Moses and Jethro hug and exit together stage left as Storyteller narrates.)

Storyteller: **Moses listened to his father-in-law's suggestions and did everything that he had said. Moses chose capable people from all Israel and set them as leaders over the people. He embraced the idea that heroes do their best work when they work together.**

Bible Story Option 2
Single Storyteller

Bible Story

Jethro Mentors Moses
Exodus 18

Hotline Verse

So let's strive for the things that bring peace and the things that build each other up. (Romans 14:19)

Hotline Tip

Heroes are called to… Work Together!

Today's Bible story, like so many, is full of ups and downs. Listen carefully. Every time you hear the word "up" stand as you're able or raise your hands above your head. And every time you hear the word "down," sit back down.

Ready? Here we go!

Moses' father-in-law, Jethro, heard about everything God had done for Moses and for God's people Israel, bringing them <u>up</u> out of Egypt.

Jethro brought Moses' wife, Zipporah, and their two sons, Gershom and Eliezer, to Moses.

Moses had put <u>down</u> a camp in the desert at God's mountain.

Jethro sent word <u>up</u> to Moses: "I, your father-in-law Jethro, am coming to you along with your wife and her two sons."

Moses went out to meet his father-in-law, and he bowed <u>down</u> and kissed him. Then Moses told his father-in-law about everything God had done to Pharaoh and to the Egyptians on Israel's behalf, all the difficulty they had on their journey, and how God had rescued them. Jethro was <u>up</u>-lifted about all the good things the Lord had done for Israel in saving them from the Egyptians' power.

Jethro said, "Bless the Lord who rescued you from Pharaoh and all those who would keep God's people <u>down</u>. Now I know the Lᴏʀᴅ is greater than all the gods, because of what happened when the Egyptians plotted against them." Later, Moses' brother, Aaron, came with all of Israel's elders to eat a meal with Moses' father-in-law in God's presence. They gobbled it <u>up</u>.

The next day Moses sat <u>down</u> as a judge for the people, while the people stood <u>up</u> around Moses from morning until evening. When Jethro saw all that Moses was doing for the people, he asked why Moses was working so hard.

Moses said, "Because the people come to me to inquire of God. When a conflict goes <u>down</u> between them, they come to me and I judge between the two of them. I also teach them God's regulations and instructions."

Jethro said to him, "What you are doing isn't good. You will end <u>up</u> totally wearing yourself out, and letting <u>down</u> these people who are with you. The work is too difficult for you. You can't do it alone.

HERO HOTLINE: Called Together to Serve God!

"Let me give you some advice. And may God be with you! Your role should be to bring <u>up</u> the disputes of the people before God. And explain the regulations and instructions to them. Let them know the way they are supposed to go and the things they are supposed to do. But you should also look for other capable people who can sit <u>down</u> as judges. Let them decide on all the minor disagreements, and only bring the major disputes to you. That will make things much easier on you and keep your life from feeling turned <u>up</u>side-<u>down</u>.

Share the load. You do this and God directs you, then you will be able to keep your energy <u>up</u>, and all these people will be able to go back to their homes much happier, rather than feeling <u>down</u>."

Moses listened to his father-in-law's suggestions and did everything that he could to follow Jethro's wise advice. Then Moses said goodbye to his father-in-law, and Jethro went back to his own country.

Bible Story
Jethro Mentors Moses
Exodus 18

Hotline Verse
So let's strive together for the things that bring peace and the things that build each other up. (Romans 14:19)

Hotline Tip
Heroes are called to… Work Together!

Bible Story
Jethro Mentors Moses
Exodus 18

Hotline Verse
So let's strive for the things that bring peace and the things that build each other up.
(Romans 14:19)

Hotline Tip
Heroes are called to…
Work Together!

Life Application

Moses had done so much to serve God by leading God's people out of slavery in Egypt. When he and the Israelites finally made it to Mount Sinai, who was happy to see him?
(Invite Heroes to respond – "His family," "His wife and children," "His father-in-law.")

And Moses was happy to see them too. But he still had so much work to do. Could he do it all by himself?
(Invite Heroes to respond, "No.")

No one can do it all by themselves. And it's exhausting to even try. Who gave Moses the great advice to share the load?
(Invite Heroes to answer, "Jethro," or "His father-in-law.")

Jethro's advice was wise. It makes me wonder sometimes if, when Jethro was younger, he tried to do it all by himself and learned the hard way he couldn't.

Jethro's advice reflects our Hotline Tip for today – Heroes are called to work together.

Let's play another game. I'll say the Hotline Tip by myself as loud as I can.

Then it will be your turn to all say it together.

My turn first.

Heroes are called to work together.

Okay, that was pretty good I think. Now it's your turn. 3-2-1-Go!
(Have Heroes chant the Hotline Tip. It will be, almost definitely, way louder.)

Wow! Working together makes it so much stronger. I want to be a part of your team! Let's do it together one more time.

Heroes are called to work together!

Wham! Bang! Pow! I love being part of a team that works together!

Active Learning
Many Grains

Divide the Heroes into small groups. Give each group:
- One small cardboard tube (half a paper towel roll)
- Two squares of tissue paper (approx. 5x5 inches)
- A rubber band
- A wooden dowel at least 1 inch in diameter. This will not work with smaller dowels.
- Table salt

Place a tissue paper square across one end of the cardboard tube. Fasten the tissue in place with a rubber band.

Push the wooden dowel through the paper.

ASK: **What happens?**
(Invite Heroes to respond "The dowel breaks right through the paper.")

SAY: **Right. There's nothing to keep that dowel from breaking right through.**
Now try this –

Place another tissue paper square across one end of the cardboard tube. Fasten the tissue in place with a rubber band.

Carefully pour about three inches of salt into the tube. Hold the tube in one hand and push the wooden dowel into the salt. Try to push hard enough to rip the tissue. Have several heroes try.

ASK: **What happens?**
(Invite Heroes to respond, "It doesn't break through.")

SAY: **The tissue is thin, and the wooden dowel is strong, but it won't rip the tissue.**

The force from the dowel is not all going straight down the tube toward the tissue.

There are many tiny spaces between all those tiny salt crystals. When you push the dowel into the salt, the crystals collide, sending the force in every direction.

Salt absorbs so much of the force that only a small part of it reaches the tissue – not enough to tear it.

It's amazing what we can do when we all choose to connect with one another and work together. We can do things that would otherwise seem impossible.

Bible Story
Jethro Mentors Moses
Exodus 18

Hotline Verse
So let's strive for the things that bring peace and the things that build each other up.
(Romans 14:19)

Hotline Tip
Heroes are called to…
Work Together!

Bible Story
Jethro Mentors Moses
Exodus 18

Hotline Verse
So let's strive for the
things that bring peace
and the things that build
each other up.
(Romans 14:19)

Hotline Tip
Heroes are called to…
Work Together!

Closing Prayer
Repeat after me each line of the following echo prayer.

Loving God,
Sometimes I might feel lost,
But I know I'm never alone,
Because you are always there
To love me,
And hold me,
And guide me safely home.
Amen.

The Magnificent Magi
Matthew 2:1-12

Materials

- Storyteller costume – could be modern attire, or all black, or a story shawl
- Bible-time attire for the magi – could be royal attire, including crowns and colorful robes
- Bible-time attire for Herod – same as above but with a different color robe/tunic
- Star Puppet – a large card stock star with craft stick. Actor playing Star can dress all in black.
- Frankincense, myrrh, and gold – these can simply be cloth bundles tied with gold ribbon
- Scroll for Herod to read from
- Storyteller Stool and stand for Storyteller
- Starry Sky background
- Hero Hotline CD and CD player (or mp3 player)

Setting the Scene

- Designate one wall to be the focal wall, serving as the backdrop for the action.
- The wall can be decorated to give the feel of a starry night sky in the background.
- The main staging area should be nice and open.
- The Storyteller's area could be to the side. There could even be a small story stool for the storyteller to sit on. Posted nearby, possibly directly overhead could be the Verse for the Week – Romans 14:19 – So let's strive for the things that bring peace and the things that build each other up.
- Additionally, there could be space on a wall where each day's Hotline Tip can be posted as it is revealed. They would look great using the superhero comic book bursts (a la "POW," "BAM," etc.) Add the Hotline Tip signs each day so they fill up the wall by the end.

Bible Story

The Magnificent Magi
Matthew 2:1-12

Hotline Verse

So let's strive for the things that bring peace and the things that build each other up.
(Romans 14:19)

Hotline Tip

Heroes are called to... Listen to God!

Bible Story
The Magnificent Magi
Matthew 2:1-12

Hotline Verse
So let's strive for the things that bring peace and the things that build each other up.
(Romans 14:19)

Hotline Tip
Heroes are called to...
Listen to God!

Teacher Tip
This Bible Background feature is a supplemental aid provided for you, the Storyteller, to give context for each session's story before you teach on it. *You may share this information with your Heroes, if desired, but it is not a recommended portion of the intended lesson.*

Bible Background

When Jesus was born, many hundreds of years after the events of Exodus with Moses and the Israelites, the descendants of the Israelites were part of the Roman Empire. As a result, they were ruled by a king who had been appointed by the caesar in Rome. This king's name was Herod, and he took threats to his rule very seriously.

Matthew 2 tells the story of some magi who came to Jerusalem in search of "the newborn king of the Jews" (Matthew 2:2). These magi—who were most likely from Persia—are established as astrologers, since they tell Herod they have seen a star heralding the arrival of the newborn king.

Herod is troubled by the magi's news. He asks for more information, saying he wants to honor the newborn king himself. But Herod has no plans to honor this king. He knows the signs the magi saw in the stars have nothing to do with him or his sons. He is only king because Rome has no interest in directly ruling Judea on their own. Furthermore, Herod is not a descendant of King David, unlike Jesus whose genealogy at the beginning of Matthew notes his royal ancestry. Therefore this child born in Bethlehem, in the city of David, has more legitimacy to Israel's throne than Herod does. This sends Herod—as well as anyone who benefits from his rule—into desperation.

Herod sends the magi on to Bethlehem with instructions to return with more information about the child. The magi arrive and meet Jesus, fall to their knees paying homage to this newborn king, and present him with gifts. This recognition of the kingship of Jesus by Gentiles in this moment marks the beginning of a new community that recognizes Jesus and praises him as Lord. It shows us that his kingship is not just for Israel, but for us all. The magi are warned in a dream not to return to Herod. They return home, but by a different route so as to not risk meeting Herod's people along the way. Herod ruled by fear, but the magi fear God and are guided to protect this newborn king by their hope in this new kingdom.

The call from God can come in many different ways. Heroes listen to God and await God's call! The cosmic signs that led the magi to Jesus should not be all that surprising to us—after all, this newborn king is the same person who will, years later, calm the winds and the seas in Matthew 8. God sends the magi back home to bear witness to the love and joy they have experienced meeting Jesus. We are called to bear witness to our own experiences under Jesus' lordship, sharing that same love and joy with others. At Hero Hotline VBS, we are learning how exciting life can be when we listen for God's call!

Story Starter

Hello, Heroes! Welcome back to Bible Story Headquarters. Today we move forward from the Old Testament to the...
(Invite Heroes to say "New Testament.")

Right, the New Testament. And today's story comes from the Gospel of Matthew. It's been a few days since we talked about the word "gospel." Do any Heroes remember what that means?
(Give Heroes an opportunity to respond. If they get stuck, simply remind them that gospel means "good news.")

Gospel means good news. And this story has plenty of good news. First, Jesus has been born. That's very good news. Second, there are people who listen to God and follow a star to see the child Jesus.

And some more good news for us is that you are getting very close to having our Hotline Verse memorized. It's the one from Romans chapter 14, verse 19 –
So let's strive for the things that bring peace and the things that build each other up.

Let's say it together, but as if it's sad news.
(Lead the Heroes to say the verse with sad voices.)

Hmm. That doesn't quite feel right, does it? Now let's say it as if it's scary news.
(Lead the Heroes to say the verse as if they're scared.)

Nope. Still not quite right. Let's do it one more time as if it were really good news!
(Lead the Heroes to say the verse with real enthusiasm.)

Wham! Bang! Pow! That was great! And now it's time for our Bible story. Here come the Magi now, as well as the "star" of our show... literally.

Bible Story
The Magnificent Magi
Matthew 2:1-12

Hotline Verse
So let's strive for the things that bring peace and the things that build each other up.
(Romans 14:19)

Hotline Tip
Heroes are called to...
Listen to God!

Bible Story

The Magnificent Magi
Matthew 2:1-12

Hotline Verse

So let's strive for the things that bring peace and the things that build each other up.
(Romans 14:19)

Hotline Tip

Heroes are called to…
Listen to God!

Bible Story Option 1
Drama

Cast

Storyteller
Magi 1
Magi 2
Magi 3
Herod
Star

Materials

- Storyteller costume – could be modern attire, or all black, or a story shawl
- Bible-time attire for the magi – could be royal attire, including crows and colorful robes
- Bible-time attire for Herod – same as above but with a different color robe/tunic
- Star Puppet – a large cardstock star with craft stick. Actor playing Star can dress all in black
- Frankincense, myrrh, and gold – these can simply be cloth bundles tied with gold ribbon
- Scroll for Herod
- Storyteller Stool and stand for Storyteller
- Starry Sky background

(Magi 1, 2, and 3 enter stage left as Storyteller narrates. Note: If magi entering from the east in your setting means flipping which side you use for their entrance, go for it!)

Storyteller: **Jesus was born in Bethlehem in the territory of Judea during the rule of King Herod. After Jesus was born, magi came from the east to Jerusalem.**

Magi 1: **The star looks even brighter tonight. I think we're getting close.**

Magi 2: **I sure hope so. This gold is really getting heavy.**

Magi 3: **Wait! Gold? You brought gold?!**

Magi 1: **I thought we all agreed on a five-shekel limit.**

Magi 2: **It's not that much gold really. Why? What did you bring?**

Magi 1: **Frankincense.**

Magi 3: **Myrrh.**

Magi 2: *(reassuringly)* **Well, those are nice gifts too.**

Magi 1: **So let me get this straight – we're bringing gifts to a child right?**

Magi 2 and 3: **Right.**

Magi 1: **And we're bringing frankincense, myrrh, and gold, right?**

Magi 2 and 3: **Right.**

Magi 1: **And none of us thought to bring a toy? Or some diapers?**

Magi 2: **Um… it's the thought that counts?**

Star: *(to Heroes)* **There are many who will call them wise, but "practical"? Maybe not so much.**
(Herod enters stage right and goes to center)

Magi 1: **Maybe we can at least put our wisdom to good use. Let's stop at this palace right here and ask that kingly-looking guy if he's seen the child.**

Magi 2: **Good idea.**
(Magi 1, 2, and 3 cross to center)

Magi 1: **Excuse me. Kingly-looking guy.**

King Herod: *(correcting)* **King Herod.**

Magi 1: **King Herod. Do you live around here?**

Herod: *(noticeably put out)* **I am the ruler of this area, the one in charge, the king. So yes, I do live around here. On the other hand you, obviously, do not.**

Magi 3: **We are on a journey to honor the newborn king of the Jews. We've seen his star in the east. Star of wonder, star of light.**

Magi 2: **Star with royal beauty bright.**

Star: **Hey, that could make a really nice song someday!**

Herod: **Did you say, "King of the Jews"?**

Magi 1, 2, and 3: **Yes!**

Herod: *(very angry)* **But I'm the…** *(walks to down stage left and says to self)* **This is very troubling. The chief priests have told about where the Christ would be born – in Bethlehem. For it is written by the prophet…** *(pulls out a scroll and reads)*

You, Bethlehem, land of Judah, by no means are you least among the rulers of Judah, because from you will come one who governs, who will shepherd my people Israel."

Bible Story
The Magnificent Magi
Matthew 2:1-12

Hotline Verse
So let's strive for the things that bring peace and the things that build each other up.
(Romans 14:19)

Hotline Tip
Heroes are called to…
Listen to God!

(angrily rolls up scroll) **That is bad news for those of us here who like everything just the way it is… with us in power.** *(Returns to Magi 1, 2, and 3, and takes on an overly-sweet tone)* **Friends, weary travelers, could I ask of you one teensy-weensy favor?**

Magi 3: **Of course.**

Magi 2: **We are happy to do what we can.**

Herod: **Wonderful. If you will go to Bethlehem, which is that way.** *(pointing to stage right)* **Go and search for the child. When you've found him, will you come let me know?**

Magi 3: **Do you have a gift for the child too?**

Herod: *(suppressing an evil grin)* **Oh, I have something for him, all right.**

Magi 1: *(sensing that something is a little off)* **Well, I think it's about time for us to head out while it's still dark enough for us to see his star. Let's go, friends.**
(Herod exits stage left. Magi 1, 2, and 3, pantomime walking in place as Storyteller narrates)

Storyteller: **When the magi left King Herod, they went; and look, the star they had seen in the east went ahead of them.**

Magi 2: **The star is even more bright and beautiful now.**

Star: **Aw thanks. I try.**

Magi 1: **It's slowing down. I think we're getting close.**

Magi 3: **Can we stop?**

Magi 1: **Stop? What for?**

Magi 3: *(a little embarrassed)* **I… um… I have to go to the bathroom.**

Magi 2: **Why didn't you go when we were at Herod's?**

Magi 3: **I didn't have to go then.**

Magi 1: **The good news is we don't have to travel any farther. See?** *(pointing)* **The star has stopped. This must be where they are.**

Magi 2: *(pointing off stage right)* **Look! It's the child.**

Magi 3: **And his mother.**
(Magi 1, 2, and 3 kneel, facing offstage right)

Magi 1: **We would like to offer you these gifts. Frankincense,** *(places frankincense on the ground)*

Magi 3: **Myrrh,** *(places myrrh on the ground)*

HERO HOTLINE: Called Together to Serve God!

Magi 2: **And gold.** (places gold on the ground)

Star: **Again, maybe not the most practical gifts, but definitely meaningful.**

Magi 1: **It was an honor to get to travel all this way, and a joy to finally see you. And now it is time for us to return home.**

Magi 3: **Can we at least rest the night? It's a long journey home.**

Magi 1: **Good idea.**
(Magi 1, 2, and 3 lie down)

Star: (singing, getting softer as the magi fall asleep)

Twinkle, twinkle little star,
How I wonder what you are,
Up above the world so high…
(Magi 1, 2, and 3 snore)

Magi 2: (pops up suddenly, and wakes up others) **Wake up, wake up! Wake up, wake up!**

Magi 1: **What is it?**

Magi 2: **I just had the strangest dream.**

Magi 3: **So did I. What was your dream about?**

Magi 2: **It was more like a warning – that we shouldn't go back the way we came.**

Magi 3: **That was in my dream too!**

Magi 1: **I had the same dream, that we shouldn't go back past Herod. It's as if Herod is…**

Magi 1, 2, and 3: **A bad guy!**

Magi 1: **We should go home by another way.**
(Magi 1, 2, and 3 rise and walk off to back of Bible Story space past Heroes)

Magi 2: **Is the star coming too?**

Magi 1: **I don't think so. But don't worry. We have all the guidance we need now. He has been born.**
(Others nod as they wave to the Star and exit out back)

Bible Story

The Magnificent Magi
Matthew 2:1-12

Hotline Verse

So let's strive for the things that bring peace and the things that build each other up.
(Romans 14:19)

Hotline Tip

Heroes are called to...
Listen to God!

Bible Story Option 2
Single Storyteller

For today's Bible story, I need your help.

Listen closely for three things. Whenever you hear one of the things you have to make a special sound. Here they are.

(Practice each one with the Heroes)

King Herod – duhn-duhn-DUHN!!!
Magi – walking feet
Star – sing "Star"

Great! Okay, here we go!

In the time of <u>King Herod</u>, after Jesus was born in Bethlehem of Judea, <u>magi</u> from the east came to Jerusalem, asking, "Where is the child who has been born king of the Jews? For we observed his <u>star</u> at its rising, and have come to honor him."

When <u>King Herod</u> heard this, he was frightened, and called together all the chief priests and scribes of the people. He asked them where the Messiah was to be born. They said, "In Bethlehem of Judea; as the prophets have written.

Then <u>King Herod</u> secretly called for the <u>magi</u> and learned from them the exact time when the <u>star</u> had appeared. Then he sent them to Bethlehem, saying, "Go and search diligently for the child; and when you have found him, come let me know so that I, too, may honor him."

When the <u>magi</u> had heard <u>King Herod</u>, they set out; and there, ahead of them, went the <u>star</u> that they had seen at its rising, until it stopped over the place where the child was. When they saw that the <u>star</u> had stopped, they were overwhelmed with joy. On entering the house, the <u>magi</u> saw the child with Mary his mother; and they knelt down and paid him homage. Then, opening their treasure chests, they offered him gifts of gold, frankincense, and myrrh. And having been warned in a dream not to return to <u>King Herod</u>, the <u>magi</u> went home to their own country by another way.

Life Application

In their culture, the magi were priests, which means they were very well respected and wealthy. They were most likely from Persia, what we know today as Iran. What did they follow to find the child Jesus?
(Invite Heroes to respond, "a star.")

How many gifts did the magi bring?
(Invite Heroes to respond, "three.")

And what were those gifts?
(Invite Heroes to respond, "Frankincense, myrrh, and gold.")

Because there were three gifts, people often assume there were three magi. But the Bible never says how many there were. Some versions of the Bible call the magi "wise men" and there are Christmas carols that refer to them as "kings," though we don't know from the Bible that they were kings. What we do know is they listened to God. When God called them to follow a star to see Jesus, they went. When God called them in a dream to go another way home, they listened.

Sometimes the call can be loud and obvious, like when Jesus called the disciples, or like when God called Moses to go to Egypt and tell Pharaoh to let God's people go free. Other times the call can be as quiet as a shining star or a whisper in the night.

Our Hotline Tip today is – Heroes are called to listen to God.

Let's whisper that together.
(Lead Heroes to whisper the Hotline Tip with you.)

Let's try that again, even softer.
(Lead Heroes.)

In a noisy world, sometimes the best thing we can do is be softer so we can better hear the voice of God calling.

Bible Story
The Magnificent Magi
Matthew 2:1-12

Hotline Verse
So let's strive together for the things that bring peace and the things that build each other up. (Romans 14:19)

Hotline Tip
Heroes are called to...
Listen to God!

Bible Story
The Magnificent Magi
Matthew 2:1-12

Hotline Verse
So let's strive for the things that bring peace and the things that build each other up.
(Romans 14:19)

Hotline Tip
Heroes are called to…
Listen to God!

Test Church Idea
After doing this activity, invite Heroes to play along with a favorite song from the Hero Hotline **Complete Music CD.**

Active Learning
Three Instruments

The Magi are often referred to as "wise men." One thing that made them very wise is that they were excellent listeners… especially to the voice of God. Here's a fun game for honing our listening skills.

Place several small percussion instruments in the center of the room. Here is a partial list:
• A rattle
• Rhythm sticks
• Sand blocks
• A triangle and beater
• Finger cymbals
• A hand drum
• A tambourine
• A wood block

Invite the Heroes to sit in a circle on the floor.

Have them close their eyes.

Choose someone to come to the center and play three different instruments, one right after the other.

Have the Heroes in the circle open their eyes and ask if someone can say, in order, which three instruments were played.

Invite an opportunity for many to play the instruments.

Closing Prayer

Repeat after me each line of the following echo prayer.

HELP ME BE SOFTER, LORD!

Help me be softer, Lord.

Help me be softer, Lord.

Help me be softer, Lord,

so I can hear you better.

Amen.

Bible Story
The Magnificent Magi
Matthew 2:1-12

Hotline Verse
So let's strive for the things that bring peace and the things that build each other up.
(Romans 14:19)

Hotline Tip
Heroes are called to…
Listen to God!

Bible Story

Unexpected Heroes Give Paul a Basket Ride
Acts 9:1-25

Hotline Verse

So let's strive for the things that bring peace and the things that build each other up.
(Romans 14:19)

Hotline Tip

Heroes are called to...
Show Grace!

Unexpected Heroes Give Paul a Basket Ride

Acts 9:10-25

Materials

- Storyteller costume – could be modern attire, or all black, or a story shawl
- Bible-time attire for Disciples 1 and 2 – robes or tunics, and sandals
- Bible-time attire for Saul – same as above but with different color robe/tunic
- Bible-time attire for Ananias – same as above
- Bible-time attire for Plotters 1 and 2 – same as Disciples 1 and 2 but with different color robe/tunic
- A large basket with a rope
- A chair for Saul
- Storyteller Stool and stand for Storyteller
- Stone wall background
- Hero Hotline CD and CD player (or mp3 player)

Setting the Scene

- Designate one wall to be the focal wall, serving as the backdrop for the action.
- The wall can be decorated to give the feel of a stone wall in the background.
- The main staging area should be nice and open.
- The Storyteller's area could be to the side. There could even be a small story stool for the storyteller to sit on. Posted nearby, possibly directly overhead could be the Verse for the Week – Romans 14:19 – So let's strive for the things that bring peace and the things that build each other up.
- Additionally, there could be space on a wall where each day's Hotline Tip can be posted as it is revealed. They would look great using the superhero comic book bursts (a la "POW," "BAM," etc.) Add the Hotline Tip signs each day so they fill up the wall by the end.

Bible Background

Jesus was not accepted by everyone as warmly as he was by the disciples who followed him or the magi who discovered him in Bethlehem. Some people, who believed that their power was challenged by Jesus' message, had Jesus arrested and killed. But on the third day after his death, Jesus was raised from the dead! Jesus' resurrection, as well as the Holy Spirit, galvanized his disciples and other followers to continue sharing his message throughout the world. This movement became the church and spread quickly in the surrounding area.

Some people opposed the church, however, believing the message shared by the church jeopardized their power the same way Jesus' ministry did. A man named Saul was one such person. Saul saw the church as a threat to the power structure that existed and sought to bring an end to this movement of Jesus followers—and often violently. However, on the way from Jerusalem to the city of Damascus, Saul encountered Jesus in a vision. In his encounter with Jesus, Saul lost his eyesight and was led by God to understand that his persecution of Jesus' followers was wrong.

All of this, including the familiar story of Saul's encounter with Jesus, serves as a backdrop for our Session 5 story, which focuses on the followers of Jesus in Damascus. As far as these disciples knew, Saul wanted them dead. One disciple, named Ananias, also receives a vision from Jesus. Jesus tells Ananias to find Saul and restore his sight. But Ananias knows about Saul, and he is wary about helping an enemy of the church. "Lord, I have heard many reports about this man. People say he has done horrible things to your holy people in Jerusalem. He's here with authority from the chief priests to arrest everyone who calls on your name" (Acts 9:13-14).

Jesus explains to Ananias that Saul will share his message with "Gentiles, kings, and Israelites." Ananias knows he must trust God's grace to transform even someone as fearsome as Saul, so he obeys. Saul's sight is restored, and he stays in Damascus with the other disciples, preaching about Jesus in the synagogues. But the tables soon turn on Saul. After preaching about Jesus to the people in Damascus, some of them began to plot to kill Saul—much like he had done before his encounter with Jesus! Jesus' disciples in Damascus had a choice: they could abandon Saul—a man who had once conspired to kill them—to fend for himself against the threat of death, or they could extend grace and help him escape the city. The disciples understood the grace shown to all of us by Jesus and extended that same grace to Saul. They snuck him out in a basket through an opening in the city wall, and Saul returned to Jerusalem to continue preaching Jesus' message.

These disciples in Damascus were called to show grace to Saul, even though they only knew of him as their enemy. Jesus calls us to show grace to everyone, too—even our enemies! It might be difficult or even scary to love our enemies. Jesus' disciples in Damascus were afraid, too. But Heroes know God is with us when we show love to everyone! Saul was transformed by his interaction with disciples who showed him grace. When we work together like the disciples in Damascus, who knows what we can accomplish?

Bible Story
Unexpected Heroes Give Paul a Basket Ride
Acts 9:1-25

Hotline Verse
So let's strive for the things that bring peace and the things that build each other up.
(Romans 14:19)

Hotline Tip
Heroes are called to…
Show Grace!

Teacher Tip
This Bible Background feature is a supplemental aid provided for you, the Storyteller, to give context for each session's story before you teach on it. *You may share this information with your Heroes, if desired, but it is not a recommended portion of the intended lesson.*

Bible Story
Unexpected Heroes Give Paul a Basket Ride
Acts 9:1-25

Hotline Verse
So let's strive for the things that bring peace and the things that build each other up.
(Romans 14:19)

Hotline Tip
Heroes are called to…
Show Grace!

Story Starter

Hello, Heroes! Welcome back for one last session at Bible Story Headquarters. This has been an action-packed week! We've had amazing stories from the Old Testament and the New Testament. Today's story comes from the New Testament right after the four Gospels. Do you remember what the word "gospel" means?
(Invite Heroes to respond, "good news.")

Right! *Gospel* means good news. After the Gospels – Matthew, Mark, Luke, and John – comes the Book of Acts. After Jesus went to heaven, his followers had a lot of work to do building the early church. Most of these were people Jesus had called, taught, prayed with, and shared meals with.

But there was a man named Saul who was not one of the original twelve. In fact he spent a lot of time arresting anyone who taught that Jesus as the Messiah/God's son. And you know what? Jesus called him anyway. Even though Jesus had gone to heaven, his love was still calling people to God's love. Saul (who is also known as Paul) would go on to write some amazing letters that are a major part of the New Testament. One of those letters even includes our Bible verse for the week - Romans chapter 14, verse 19 –
So let's strive for the things that bring peace and the things that build each other up.

Let's say it together three times in a row, first softly, then medium loud, then very loud. Ready? Here we go.
(Lead the Heroes to chant the Bible verse three times.)

Wham! Bang! Pow! That was amazing. You know what else is amazing? Grace – a special love from God that isn't earned or deserved. It's a love that's freely given because God is, well, God.

Bible Story Option 1
Drama

Cast:
- Storyteller
- Saul
- Ananias
- Disciple 1
- Disciple 2
- Plotter 1
- Plotter 2

Materials:
- Storyteller costume – could be modern attire, or all black, or a story shawl
- Bible-time attire for Disciples 1 and 2 – robes or tunics, and sandals
- Bible-time attire for Saul – same as above but with different color robe/tunic
- Bible-time attire for Ananias – same as above
- Bible-time attire for Plotters 1 and 2 – same as Disciples 1 and 2 but with different color robe/tunic
- A large basket with a rope
- A chair for Saul
- Storyteller Stool and stand for Storyteller
- Stone wall background

(Ananias enters stage left)

Storyteller: **In Damascus there was a certain disciple named Ananias. The Lord spoke to him in a vision, "Ananias!"**

Ananias: **Yes, Lord.**

Storyteller: **The Lord instructed him, "Go to Judas' house on Straight Street and ask for a man from Tarsus named Saul. He is praying. In a vision he has seen a man named Ananias enter and put his hands on him to restore his sight."**

Ananias: *(directly to Storyteller)* **Whoa! Saul of Tarsus?! I've heard about this guy! People say he has done some seriously mean things to your holy people in Jerusalem!**

Storyteller: **Hey Ananias, I'm the Storyteller. I'm just telling you what God's words are.**

Ananias: **But Saul's here with authority from the chief priests to arrest everyone who calls on your name.**

Storyteller: **The Lord replied, "Go! This man is the agent I have chosen to**

Bible Story
Unexpected Heroes Give Paul a Basket Ride
Acts 9:1-25

Hotline Verse
So let's strive for the things that bring peace and the things that build each other up.
(Romans 14:19)

Hotline Tip
Heroes are called to…
Show Grace!

Pronunciation Guide
Ananias- AN-nuh-ny-us

carry my name before Gentiles, kings, and Israelites."

Ananias: **Okay, I'm going.** (Crosses over to stage right. Saul enters stage right, sits in a chair, and closes his eyes.) **The Lord sure shows a lot of grace towards Saul. I will trust in the Lord's goodness. This must be the house. Excuse me. Are you Saul?**

Saul: **Yes, I'm Saul.**

Ananias: **I am Ananias. The Lord has instructed me to place hands on you. You aren't going to bite me, are you?**

Saul: **No.**

Ananias: **Are you going to kick me?**

Saul: **No.**

Ananias: **Are you going to be mean to me?**

Saul: **Not at all.**

Ananias: **Okay. Then here we go.** (places hand on Saul's shoulder) **Brother Saul, Jesus, who appeared to you on the way as you were coming here - he sent me so that you could see again and be filled with the Holy Spirit.**
(Saul opens eyes and looks around wonder-struck)

Saul: **Hey. I can see again! Thank you, Ananias.**
(As Storyteller narrates, Saul stands and moves to center stage. Ananias follows. Plotters 1 and 2 enter stage left and stand to the left of Saul. Disciples 1 and 2 enter stage right and stand to the right of Saul.)

Storyteller: **Saul got up and was baptized. After eating, he regained his strength. He stayed with the disciples in Damascus for several days. Right away, he began to preach about Jesus in the synagogues.**

Saul: (to Plotters 1 and 2) **Jesus is God's Son. He is God's Son!**

Disciple 1: (to Disciple 2) **Saul really is a man on a mission.**

Disciple 2: (to Disciple 1) **It's hard to believe this is the same guy who was making life hard on anyone in Jerusalem who called the Lord's name.**

Saul: **Jesus came to teach, to heal, to work miracles!**

Disciple 1: **It's pretty inspiring how God can transform someone for good.**

Disciple 2: **Yeah, but I don't think everyone finds it so inspiring.** (indicating to Plotters 1 and 2)

Plotter 1: (to Plotter 2) **Just who in the world does this "Saul" think he is?!**

Plotter 2: (to Plotter 1) **Yeah! I thought he came here to make prisoners of any who are followers of the**

way. But now he's acting just like them.

Plotter 1: **He keeps going on about Jesus as if Jesus was some kind of hero.**

Plotter 2: **I know. Hearing things I don't one hundred percent agree with really gets on my nerves.**

Plotter 1: **Maybe we could get rid of Saul.**

Plotter 2: **By "get rid of him" do you mean like walk him to the edge of town and wave nicely as he walks off into the sunset?**

Plotter 1: **I mean** (with a menacing tone) **get rid of him.**

Plotter 2: (realizing) **Ooh! I like your idea better.** (bad guy laugh) **Mwah-ah-ah!**
(Plotter 1 joins in)

Plotters 1 and 2: **Mwah-ah-ah! Mwah-ah-ah!**

Plotter 1: **Okay. Let's sneak to the city gates and keep watch. Whenever we see Saul come by... we'll shut him up for good.**

Plotters 1 and 2: (whispering as they tiptoe to far downstage left) **Mwah-ah-ah. Mwah-ah-ah.**

Disciple 1: **Saul, did you hear that?**

Saul: **Sorry, I guess I kind of got carried away with sharing the good news about Jesus. Hear what?**

Disciple 2: **Some people don't like what you have to say. There's a plot to get rid of you for good.**

Saul: **Aw, man! And just when I was starting to do good guy stuff.**

Disciple 1: **Look, some bad guys have a plot, but we can have a plot too, a good guy plot, a helpful plot.**

Disciple 2: **Instead of "plot" let's call ours a plan. That's got more of a heroic ring to it.**

Disciple 1: **Perfect, a helpful plan.**

Saul: **Great! So what is this helpful plan?**

Disciples 1 and 2: (looking at each other, stumped) **Um...**

Disciple 1: **Hey I've got an idea! Remember how baby Moses was saved by being placed in a basket and set gently in the river?**

Disciple 2: **Of course! We covered that in Session 2!**

Disciple 1: **Wait. What?!**

Disciple 2: (slyly to the Heroes) **Oh, nothing.**

Disciple 1: **Anyway, people are waiting for Saul at the gate to the city. What if we put Saul in a basket and lowered him through an opening in the wall.**

Saul: **That's a great idea.**

Disciple 2: **Hey! Here's a basket that looks just big enough.**

Disciple 1: **We could use all the muscle we can get to lower Saul down. Ananias?**

Ananias: **I'm in! Let's do this!**
(Ananias, Disciples 1 and 2, and Saul go to upstage left where they are behind Plotters 1 and 2. Plotters 1 and 2 keep facing forward so as not to see the others.)

Disciple 1: **Okay, there they are waiting to get you. Saul, climb into the basket.** (Saul does) **Now let's lower him down.**
(Ananias and Disciples 1 and 2 pantomime lowering Saul down)

Saul: (enjoying the ride a bit too much) **Hey look, everyone! I'm Baby Moses!**

Ananias and Disciples 1 and 2: **Ssh.**

Saul: **Oh right.** (finally "lowered" to the ground, in stage whisper) **Thank you, friends. You really are heroes.**

Ananias and Disciples 1 and 2: (stage whispering) **So are you.**

HERO HOTLINE: Called Together to Serve God!

Bible Story Option 2

Single Storyteller

Today's Bible story is a body tag story. Listen carefully. Every time you hear me mention a part of the body, touch that part until you hear the next one.

Ready? Here we go!

In Damascus there was a disciple named Ananias. The Lord spoke to him in a vision, "Ananias!"

Ananias's raised his <u>head</u>. He answered, "Yes, Lord."

The Lord instructed him to get on his <u>feet</u>. "Go to Judas' house on Straight Street and ask for a man from Tarsus named Saul. He is praying. In a vision he has seen a man named Ananias enter and put <u>hands</u> on him to restore his sight."

Ananias countered, "Lord, my <u>ears</u> have heard about him. People say he has done horrible things to your holy people in Jerusalem. He's here with authority from the chief priests to arrest everyone who calls on your name." The Lord replied, "Go! This man is the agent I have chosen to carry my name before Gentiles, kings, and Israelites. I will show him how much he must suffer for the sake of my name."

Ananias went to the house. He placed his <u>hands</u> on Saul and said, "Brother Saul, the Lord sent me—Jesus, who appeared to you on the way as you were coming here. He sent me so that you could see again and be filled with the Holy Spirit." Instantly, flakes fell from Saul's <u>eyes</u>, and he could see again. He got up and was baptized. After eating, he regained his strength. He stayed with the disciples in Damascus for several days. Right away, he began using his <u>mouth</u> to preach about Jesus in the synagogues. "He is God's Son," he declared.

Everyone who heard him was baffled. They shrugged their <u>shoulders</u> and questioned each other, "Isn't he the one who was wreaking havoc among those in Jerusalem who called on his name? Hadn't he come here to take those same people as prisoners to the chief priests?"

But Saul grew stronger and stronger in his faith. He confused the Jews who lived in Damascus by proving what he believed with all his <u>heart</u>—that Jesus is the Christ.

After this had gone on for some time, the Jews hatched a plot to get rid of Saul for good. However, he found out about their scheme. They were keeping watch at the city gates around the clock so they could overtake him. But his disciples took him by night, and with all the strength their <u>arms</u> could muster, they lowered Saul in a basket through an opening in the city wall.

Bible Story
Unexpected Heroes Give Paul a Basket Ride
Acts 9:1-25

Hotline Verse
So let's strive for the things that bring peace and the things that build each other up. (Romans 14:19)

Hotline Tip
Heroes are called to… Show Grace!

Pronunciation Guide
Ananias- AN-nuh-ny-us

Bible Story

Unexpected Heroes Give
Paul a Basket Ride
Acts 9:1-25

Hotline Verse

So let's strive for the
things that bring peace
and the things that build
each other up.
(Romans 14:19)

Hotline Tip

Heroes are called to…
Show Grace!

Life Application

Was Saul originally trying to help God's people?
(Invite Heroes to answer, "No. He wanted to put them in jail.")

Saul wanted to punish anyone who followed the way of Jesus. But Jesus still chose to work through Saul. When the voice of Jesus came to Saul and asked him to change his ways, Saul temporarily lost his sight. Who did Jesus send to lay hands on Saul?
(Invite Heroes to respond, "Ananias.")

Ananias, like many of the disciples, was afraid of Saul. But Jesus showed grace – unearned love – to Saul. Saul was transformed by this grace and became one of the great leaders for the early church, spreading the good news of Jesus. Was everyone happy about this new development?
(Invite Heroes to respond, "No. Some in the community wanted him gone for good.")

Once again, grace saved Saul. It was the grace of the disciples that motivated them to save Saul's life by lowering him in the basket beyond the view of those who hated him. Believers everywhere would come to know Saul as Paul, who did so much good work for God. What do you think would have happened if the disciples hadn't helped rescue Saul?

Has someone ever forgiven you even when you didn't feel you deserved it? Has anyone ever done something kind for you, or given you a nice gift even though you didn't feel you had earned it?

How did that feel?

Now imagine how good it must feel to be the one giving the gift, the one showing grace.

Our Hotline Tip for today is – Heroes are called to show grace.

Let's say that together with kindness in our hearts.
(Lead Heroes to chant the Hotline Tip.)

Grace transformed Saul. Grace transforms us. Grace can transform the world!

Active Learning
One Left

Divide the Heroes into pairs.

Give each pair 15 small stones or marbles.

This is a game called One Left.

Here's how to play:
- **Players take turns removing pebbles.**
- **Each turn, you can remove 1, 2, or 3 pebbles. Your choice. But when it's your turn, you must take at least one pebble.**
- **The goal is to never be the one stuck taking the last pebble, but rather to be the one who leaves the last pebble for your fellow player.**

Invite the Heroes to play several rounds.

God gives us all enough, if only we'll share. And because God gives grace so freely, shouldn't we also give grace to one another?

Bible Story
Unexpected Heroes Give
Paul a Basket Ride
Acts 9:1-25

Hotline Verse
So let's strive for the
things that bring peace
and the things that build
each other up.
(Romans 14:19)

Hotline Tip
Heroes are called to...
Show Grace!

Materials
- small stones or marbles,
  8 per child
- plastic bags or small
  baskets for stones or
  marbles

Bible Story

Unexpected Heroes Give
Paul a Basket Ride
Acts 9:1-25

Hotline Verse

So let's strive for the
things that bring peace
and the things that build
each other up.
(Romans 14:19)

Hotline Tip

Heroes are called to…
Show Grace!

Closing Prayer

Repeat after me each line of this rhyming prayer.

Some of us are short.
Some of us are tall
Some of us perform ballet.
Some of us play ball.

Everyone is different,
But one thing stays the same –
God loves every one of us
And knows us all by name.
Amen.